MANUAL

(THE WAY MEN THINK)

DEDICATION

To every woman who truly desires to understand that precious man in her life.

CONTENTS

WHY ARE MEN LIKE THIS?

I have been a pastor and marriage counsellor for over twenty years and in all my years of counselling women, I have found a common denominator in the complaints women make concerning the men in their lives; most women have no clue how men think and this can be very frustrating for women. My desire is that in reading this book MANUAL, it would be a guide to help you understand the man you are with or are married to and the way he thinks.

Without the right knowledge, it would take a lifetime or more to understand a man—as simple as he is. Interestingly, most women would readily agree that men are generally not as complex as women are; yet they cannot seem to figure out why they do not understand men. This knowledge gap is the underlying factor behind the emotional hurts women experience in relationships.

When asked why I focus more on enlightening women during relationship seminars my answer is usually quite simple: women are the ones most affected by the consequences of a bad relationship. Women get hurt when a relationship goes sour, they feel used when sex is involved, they can get pregnant, go through the pains of aborting an unwanted pregnancy or generally just put their lives on hold to raise the child if they go through with the pregnancy, while dealing with the stigma of being a single mother. While the man in most cases, would totally disconnect, stop calling, stop visiting and move on with his life like nothing ever happened. This usually comes as a shock to most women because they do not understand that men function differently from women.

The truth is, most men can be understood. However, just as it is with your phones, television sets and other sophisticated technological devices, you will need a manual to figure him out: a guide to his operating system. The best way to fully help you understand men is for me to present him to you as a sophisticated device that you want but need a manual to handle. The purpose of every manual is to help you understand, manage and maximize the device it came with. A manual will help you understand the accessories that work best with a device while warning you of the possible hazards to the device. From a good manual, you can also get advice on troubleshooting and maintenance. The man you are with or already married to is a product manufactured and assembled by God; he is God's device.

The principles adapted in this book are a mix of God's instructions and personal experiences as a relationship coach. I'd like you to have an open heart while reading this book because some of the things you will be reading may be hard to swallow. They are not the regular things your girlfriends will tell you. You need to realize that the best person to give you advice about a man is a man because men understand each other better.

Men are not like women so you cannot relate with a man based on how you feel or the way you relate with your female friends. A man is different from a woman in so many ways. His priorities, values, and perspectives are very different. I'll give you an example. I bought a goldfish for my children and it came with the instruction, “Feed once daily.” So, we kept strictly to that. Not too long after we got them, we had a guest who stayed at our house for a while. When she realized that we fed the fish once every day, she could not believe it. She must have thought to herself, “Wow! You mean you just feed this beautiful tiny fish once a day? But, why? That is so cruel. They will starve! Even children need to eat at least three times a day.” So, she went ahead to feed the fish more than was prescribed because she loved it. What do you think came out of all that love she felt for the fish? Of course, the fish died. She literally killed it with love. Dealing with a man is exactly like this. You can love him all you want but if you don't relate with him according to certain principles, you will not get the best out of him. It is that simple.

A few years ago, I was about to buy a dog and was told that I needed to be trained on how to relate with the dog. To be honest, I found that very amusing because I have had other dogs in the past. I told them not to worry that I would be fine. I really believed that I would be. You see, I had a Basenji as a child so I was confident that I could handle any dog. Fortunately, they were quick to inform me that what I was about to buy did not belong to a breed I was used to. In fact, this particular dog was a Pit-bull: not a calm breed at all. A dog that is capable of killing a human being. Dogs are generally from the wolf family and wolves are what we call pack animals. Pack animals are animals that move in groups and determine who leads the pack by who is strongest and not by election or emotions. The strongest animal in the pack automatically leads the pack. So, I had to be trained on how to deal with this dog so that it would submit to my leadership.

It is the same way with men. Just like they had to train me, you also need to be trained on how to relate with your husband or fiancé. A good understanding of the man you are with or about to get married to is very important to your happiness and general wellbeing.

However, let me warn you ahead that this book will totally change how you see men. If you had fairy tale notions about him being Mr. perfect and always saying and doing the right things. Well, simply brace yourself because I will be showing you the real picture of the average man – flaws and all. It will also require you to make some adjustments that you may not like or understand at first. It will require time and patience but when you finally do make these adjustments, your relationship with the man in your life will be on what I call “auto cruise.” It would be almost seamless.

Disclaimer

As with everything in life, where there is a rule there is usually an exception. So, your husband or fiancé may not fit exactly one hundred percent into how I would describe men in this book. And this is because there will always be people who are different from the regular folks. So, if you find that some of the things, I discussed in this book do not completely apply to your man or your situation, it's alright. My aim is to give a general overview of how men think and behave.

However, let me give you a few reasons why your man may be different:

Training changes men

Some men are fortunate to be raised differently from societal norms, so they do not follow their natural instincts. They have been trained and conditioned to behave differently. If for instance, a man grew up in a home where he was taught to do house chores like washing dishes and keeping the house clean just like his sisters, he wouldn't get married and expect his wife to do everything or feel like helping out with chores makes him less of a man. He will act differently from the man who saw his mom treated like the family slave all her life. He has been conditioned to treat a woman better irrespective of the situation or circumstances he finds himself in.

Spirituality changes men

An active relationship with God will change any man. Men who pattern their lives after God, allowing God's Word to decide what is right and wrong for them will naturally act differently. So, if your husband has given his life to Christ and by the help of the Holy Spirit has a renewed mind, you will observe that he lives above the natural tendencies of men. A man who is in touch with his spiritual source will be conscious of the fact that his wife or the woman in his life is God's child and will treat her with the utmost respect. His reverence for God would also keep him from doing anything contrary to God's laws; he is the kind of man that you wouldn't need to convince that premarital sex is sin and even if he struggles with it, he is more likely to overcome. His response to the women in his life would be that of kindness and tenderness.

My prayer is that as you read this book, you will receive the grace to let go of every wrong mindset as you embrace God's wisdom for a better relationship or marriage.

KNOWING YOUR MAN

Before you relate with anything, you must first understand the psychology of it.

Almost everyone who had the privilege of attending high school can label the anatomy of a man. However, being able to point out the different parts of a man is not the same as knowing a man. To know a man, you need to understand how he processes information. There is a reason why the man in your life behaves the way he does. The good news is that all men are not so different from each other. At their core, they mostly think alike. So how do men think? What makes them so different? Why is it that you can't read them half of the time? I believe that once you get these few traits that cuts across most men, you will start to get a hang of how to relate better with the man in your life.

Men Do Not Think Relationally

This perhaps is one of the hardest truths I have had to tell any woman. Romantic relationships do not matter to men as much as they do to women. In fact, the average man might never attend a relationship seminar or read a book on relationships. He believes that if he can work and make enough money to provide for the woman in his life, he will have a good marriage.

On the other hand, as a woman, your creator made you more relationally minded. You see, when God made Adam, he was alone in the garden and had nobody to talk to. That's why men would rather be left alone with their thoughts. Most times, when a man gets married, he has to adjust from life as a single man to life as a married man. A man can actually be with you and not talk to you because he is preoccupied with his thoughts. The temptation for most women at such times is to ask, "What are you thinking?" because she thinks it will help them bond. Well, that's the wrong question because you would have succeeded in throwing him off, leaving him even more confused thinking which of his thoughts to let you in on. Men are not as expressive as women. We would rather think than talk.

Another thing to note is that the first thing Adam saw when he was created was work. It was his first emotional attachment and first love. Eve, on the other hand, saw a man as the very first thing when she arrived on the scene. From then till today, one of the easiest ways to get a woman's attention is to talk about men. Most times, a woman would put in a lot of effort in the way she dresses or long hours at the hair salon just to be attractive to a man. Men are not like that.

Personally, God is my relationship mentor. I understand relationships better as I observe how God relates with men and women in the Bible. Let's take a look at ***Genesis chapters 2 and 3.*** Adam and Eve disobeyed God in the Garden of Eden and God had to discipline them. He disciplined Adam in an area that mattered most to him. He said to him, '***You'll be working in pain all your lifelong. The ground will sprout thorns and weeds, you'll get your food the hard way,***' Genesis 3:18 (The Message) God didn't say to Adam 'From now on, it will be very difficult for you to find a woman...' No. God touched him where he knew he would feel it the most. The moment He touched his work and inevitably, his finances, He had Adam's full attention. Similarly, when God was going to address the woman, He didn't say to her, 'You will sweat to make money.' He simply told her '***You'll want to please your husband, but he'll lord it over you.***' He also told her, '***I'll multiply your pains in childbirth; you'll give birth to your babies in pain.***' Genesis 3:16 (The Message) He touched her relationships and family where He knew she would feel it the most. God understands that men are work-oriented while women are more relational and family-oriented. A man will gladly give up his relationship for work or his marriage for money. I have counseled a couple of women whose husbands have instructed them to commit adultery in exchange for money. And I cannot count the number of men that divorce their wives to marry a strange woman outside the country so they can get the relevant papers they need for their foreign passports or resident permits.

Men and women are so different. A man can live out the rest of his life happily without a relationship, however, what he does want is **sex**. There are married men who operate in the '*I just want sex*' mode. These men enjoy sex in their marriage, but they are not in a 'relationship' with their wives. They both live in the same house and raise their children together but there is no real relationship between them. All they have in common is their children and great sex. Relationally, they are worlds apart. You must understand that in the average man's mind, a woman is quite dispensable. This is especially true for a carnal man. He can trade his woman for anything more beneficial at the snap of a finger. Sex is of utmost importance to him and sadly, he can get it with as many people as he wants in the world we live in today. What does this tell you? *Except a man is trained, except a man submits to mentorship, except his mind is renewed, getting involved in a relationship with him can be very difficult for you.*

From the chapters we read earlier, you would notice that when the first woman, Eve, came into the world, the first thing she encountered was a man and a relationship with that man; Adam proposed to her immediately.

***And Adam said, This is now bone of my bones, and flesh of my flesh: she shall be called Woman, because she was taken out of Man.-Genesis 2:23* [KJV]**

From that moment till today, marriage has been more important to a woman than it is to a man. Even women who "seemingly" do not care about relationships, right inside of them hidden somewhere, is the need to be with someone. Feminism, in its original sense, is good but today, some women who probably have been hurt by men have changed it into a movement of women who believe they do not need men and can do without men. The truth is, we can't do without each other. We all need each other.

As a woman, your Creator made you for relationships. *You need a man.* Do not deny it. Do not fight it instead come to terms with it. It is the natural order. I mentioned earlier that there is always an exception to every rule so it is not out of order to find a few women who cannot be bothered about relationships. Nevertheless, for the bulk of women on this planet, relationships are vital and much of your happiness will come from your relationships being healthy. I cannot count the number of women who are willing to throw away their careers, sacrifice their academics, and part with other valuables in order to get or keep a man. This is very common, and it is simply because that is how women are wired, but men are not wired that way.

Men Are Not Expressive

As I mentioned earlier, men are not as expressive as women. The average man is not good at communicating. He would rather take his time to think things through than talk about them. Especially in parts of the world like Africa, it is almost forbidden for men to talk about their feelings especially to a woman. It is a very awkward, vulnerable and uncomfortable place for any man to be and men hate to be vulnerable.

It is a fact that men really do not like to show their emotions. That is why most men actually find it extremely difficult to say the words, '*I am sorry*'. Saying 'I am sorry' puts him in a vulnerable place and he would rather carry on talking about something else, crack jokes or play with you like nothing ever happened. That is his way of apologizing. Over time, he could and should learn to apologize but his natural instinct is to avoid vulnerability. The general principle is this; when a couple have a misunderstanding, and the man starts to joke or communicate with the woman in order to get her attention, that may be his version of an apology. As a woman wisdom would be to know this, recognize it and accept it in that moment and at a later time which you consider a good time, when everything is back to normal and you are having a neutral conversation, you can chip it in that you would have preferred a verbal apology. This is far better than carrying on with malice or answering him with monosyllables when he's trying to talk to you or get your attention just because you did not hear the actual words, “I am sorry.” Interestingly, that is what most women would naturally do because women don't just ignore issues, they would rather talk about them.

Please note that it is not wise to insist on an apology when the fight is still on. Most men will consider it a confrontation and men are warriors. If you confront a man, he will take you as an enemy but if you stand by him, he will take you as an ally. You can tell him nicely when things are settled that the next time you have a disagreement and he realizes that he is wrong, you would really prefer that he verbally apologize to you. This is a way of coaching him on how to relate with you better. If he does it again, patiently repeat the process until he gets it. Even I had to learn this from my wife. Whenever I upset her, I would find ways to make her laugh but never actually say the words, “I am sorry.” She found this strange but kept on teaching me that a verbal apology would have been better appreciated. I also tried to teach her that men don't find it easy to apologize. Even with my three-year-old son, it's no different. Whenever his sisters offend him and we tell them to apologize to him, they do it without giving it a second thought but when the tables are turned and he has to apologize to them, he would rather throw tantrums or fall on the ground in tears. No one taught him that. It is just normal and often accepted behavior among men – when men have fights no one sees the need to give or receive a formal apology – we just carry on talking about other things. My wife and I had to consciously teach our son that apologizing doesn't negate his manhood. A couple of people think that this behavior is based on societal influence. It is not necessarily so; it is just how men are. You need to understand this and start putting it to work for your own husband. You do not have to train all the men in the world, you only have to work on your own husband.

Men Are Not Externally Motivated

Men and women are not motivated the same way. Women are externally motivated while men are internally motivated which is why appealing to a man's emotions or feelings is not the best way to motivate him. For instance, if a man does not like you, no matter the sacrifice you make for him it will not make him change his mind. He may take advantage of all that you are doing for him and actually hang around you, but he will not start to like you that way.

Men are hunters. It's the way they are wired. It doesn't have the same effect if it is simply handed to him. The chase is taken away and men need the chase; they need to hunt. When a man really wants something, he goes for it. This means that regardless of what is going on in his environment, he will do what he needs to do to get what he wants. Jacob in the Bible is a good example. He was willing to work for fourteen (14) years for the woman he loved. He served the first seven years but was given another woman, so he served another seven years to get the one he loved.

So Jacob served seven years to get Rachel, but they seemed like only a few days to him because of his love for her. - Genesis 29:20 [NIV]
And he went in also unto Rachel, and he loved also Rachel more than Leah, and served with him yet seven other years. - Genesis 29:30 [KJV]

Women are typically externally motivated, so they often assume that men are also externally motivated. A woman who does not initially like a man will grow to start liking him if he starts doing all the right things. But you will not achieve much when you try to motivate a man that way. You can buy him a car, pay his bills, offer free sex and even take care of his parents and he still won't like you. This is because he is not motivated by external factors. The average man is selfish and will only do things if it somehow favors him and wouldn't even mind if you get hurt in the process.

I once counselled a husband who got into a serious adulterous relationship with a strange woman that lasted for quite some time. Thankfully, God intervened; he ended that relationship and got back with his wife. A short while after that, we met and I asked him, 'Hope you are done with that lifestyle? And he replied, 'Yes, Pastor. You know I am building a new business, so I have to be careful.' Interestingly, he did not stop because he was hurting his wife and putting his family at risk. No, he stopped because it was affecting *his* business. He was spending a lot and was being distracted by the other woman in his life. I told you a man would not do anything that doesn't favor him. So even though he wanted to keep having multiple sex partners, he made a decision to stop for his own good not for his wife or family and definitely not because he felt compassion for her.

In a man's world, by this I mean the unsaved man, having multiple sex partners makes him feel like a real man. The unsaved man actually looks forward to it. But, in a woman's world, it is the fact that she is the only one for her man that makes it great and special. You need to know that no matter how much a man cares about you, he simply cannot understand how much cheating on you really hurts you. He can see your tears and distress, but he cannot relate with the depths of pain and heartbreak you feel, and this is simply because he is not motivated by emotions.

Men Are Not Emotional

Most men are not emotional. I truly wish women could understand this. Men give in more to logic and reasoning than emotions, which is why *love fights* and other emotional gimmicks do not work so well with men. If an average woman is 90 percent emotionally developed, then the average man is about 9% emotionally developed.

And I'll tell you why. As a child, a girl would play with dolls, plates and pots. With these items, she is trying to care for and nurture someone other than herself. It is part of her nature and how she is wired to be a nurturer. This tells you how women are conditioned to be from a very tender age. A boy, on the other hand, would rather play with guns and football. He has a lot of energy and would rather exercise that strength on physical things he can throw, kick around or shoot at with his toy gun.

As both sexes grow into adulthood, these tendencies grow as well. Men grow to be more logical and practical in their dealings while women are still largely emotional and caring. When it comes to giving and receiving gifts, for a woman it is the thought that counts but a man would want you to give him a practical and important gift that he can use. If you buy a pen for a woman, she will go "Awww...You thought of me. You bought me a pen. It is so beautiful." Try getting the same pen for a man as a gift and he would ask you, "What do you want me to write?"

That is why as a woman if you are going to enjoy a good relationship with a man you must strive to develop yourself intellectually and not just emotionally. The average man cannot always connect with you on an emotional level or feel your emotional pains. For instance, when a woman is pregnant or going through her monthly cycle, the average man can't relate to that. He can tell that you are going through something by looking at you, but he has no clue what it is or the level of discomfort you have to endure because he is not emotional. Emotions do not come naturally to a man and that is why God had to instruct him to love his wife.

And to the husbands, you are to demonstrate love for your wives with the same tender devotion that Christ demonstrated to us, his bride. For he died for us, sacrificing himself. - Ephesians 5:25[TPT]

God didn't have to instruct the woman on this because a woman loves naturally. A girl has clear pictures of how her wedding will be from childhood, but a boy cannot be bothered with that. He has no dreams of settling down. This is another reason why developing yourself beyond just emotions is very important as it will help you bridge the gap that exists between men and women. It will also help you add value to your man's life.

Men Do Not Like To Be Disrespected

One of the basic needs of every man is respect. I do not mean you should submit to every man you come across. No, I am referring to your own husband. Respecting your husband has nothing to do with how respectable he is or not. You are to respect him because God says you should. Even when your husband is not very respectable, you will be amazed that when you start respecting him, he will step up. Respecting your husband is one of the ways you honor God. It also helps God reach him better.

In the same way, you wives must accept the authority of your husbands. Then, even if some refuse to obey the Good News, your godly lives will speak to them without any words. They will be won over by observing your pure and reverent lives. - 1st Peter 3:1 [NLT]

This is a commandment in the same way that God commanded the men to love their wives, even when they are not lovable. Think about it, if you disagree with your boss at the office over something and you wanted to express your opinion, you would not shout at him or speak to him rudely. You would be as polite as possible, stick to the issue at hand and not attack his person. You would be very mindful of your words and tone. This tells you that if you really respect the person you are in a relationship with, there would be less heated arguments between both of you. That is why the ideal thing is to marry someone you genuinely respect and can respect.

Respect is a necessity for every man. If you are going to get the best out of him then respect is the easiest way. You can get a man to literally change anything for you once you can treat him respectfully or speak to him with high regard. All over the Bible, there were examples of women who understood this principle and the effect it had on their relationships. The Bible tells us that Sarah called Abraham her master.

For example, Sarah obeyed Abraham and called him her master. You are her true children if you do right and don't let anything frighten you. - 1st Peter 3:6 [CEV]

I don't think God expects you to go around calling your husband "master" except that works for both of you. I think he's just trying to emphasize the power of respect in a marriage. Another amazing woman in the Bible was Abigail the wife of Nabal. She showed David so much respect that David never forgot about her. She made him feel like a king even though he hadn't ascended the throne at the time.

When Abigail saw David, she quickly got off her donkey and bowed down before David with her face to the ground. She fell at his feet and said: "Pardon your servant, my lord, and let me speak to you; hear what your servant has to say. Please pay no attention, my lord, to that wicked man Nabal. He is just like his name—his name means Fool, and folly goes with him. And as for me, your servant, I did not see the men my lord sent." Please forgive your servant's presumption. The Lord your God will certainly make a lasting dynasty for my lord, because you fight the Lord's battles, and no wrongdoing will be found in you as long as you live. Even though someone is pursuing you to take your life, the life of my lord will be bound securely in the bundle of the living by the Lord your God, but the lives of your enemies he will hurl away as from the pocket of a sling. When the Lord has fulfilled for my lord every good thing he promised concerning him and has appointed him ruler over Israel, my lord will not have on his conscience the staggering burden of needless bloodshed or of having avenged himself. And when the Lord your God has brought my lord success, remember your servant. David said to Abigail, "Praise be to the Lord, the God of Israel, who has sent you today to meet me. May you be blessed for your good judgment and for keeping me from bloodshed this day and from avenging myself with my own hands." - 1st Samuel 25:23-31 [NIV]

Once he heard her husband died, he came back to marry her.

When David heard that Nabal was dead, he said, "Praise be to the Lord, who has upheld my cause against Nabal for treating me with contempt. He has kept his servant from doing wrong and has brought Nabal's wrongdoing down on his own head." Then David sent word to Abigail, asking her to become his wife. 40 His servants went to Carmel and said to Abigail, "David has sent us to you to take you to become his wife." She bowed down with her face to the ground and said, "I am your servant and am ready to serve you and wash the feet of my Lord's servants."

Abigail quickly got on a donkey and, attended by her five female servants, went with David's messengers and became his wife. - 1st Samuel 25:39-41 [NIV]

In Ephesians 5:33, God clearly defined the ingredients to ensure a successful marriage and the woman's instruction was simply to respect the man.

However, let each man of you [without exception] love his wife as [being in a sense] his very own self;

and let the wife see that she respects and reverences her husband [that she notices him, regards him, honors him, prefers him, venerates, and esteems him; and that she defers to him, praises him, and loves and admires him exceedingly]. - Ephesians 5:33 [AMPC]

Respect is an essential and innate need of every man. God made man so He understands how important it is for a man to be respected. Once a man feels like he is not respected or valued, he feels like he is at war and he brings out all the weapons in his arsenal. You become the enemy and he will do whatever it takes to get back at you.

Men are Warriors

Silent treatment is a weapon often used by men to get at women when they are upset. It is not unusual to see a woman at her wits end wondering how to get through to a husband or fiancé who is giving her the silent treatment. At times like this, you need to know what to do. So, here's my advice: ***give him some space.*** If you keep coming to him every day trying to get him to talk, he will take it as an attack and will withdraw even further from you. So, give him some space let him calm down. When he is a bit relaxed, find something that he likes to discuss and talk to him about it. Be genuinely interested in things that catch his interest. Let it not be easy for him to get through a day without needing to speak with you. You will discover that you will not even know when you start talking to each other again.

Some women in a bid to get a man's attention when he is giving them the silent treatment put up ***love fights.*** Love fights are those emotional fights you engage in with someone or people you love, knowing that you will eventually make up afterward. Women are actually very fond of this. However, in a man's world, *love* and *fight* are two words that do not go together. He only understands *fight* so while you are pretending to be angry so you can get his attention, to him, you have declared war and he is willing to fight to the end. At this point, if he is angry with you it is real and if he is keeping malice with you, that is also real. If you had threatened him that you will never talk to him again while you were both having a *love fight*, he will take you at your word and hold you to it. He will not talk to you and he has no intention of losing to you so be prepared for malice.

I remember a couple I counselled and had to intervene in their marriage at some point. During one of their love fights, the woman told her husband to leave the house and the man packed his bags and was gone for weeks. We had to intervene for him to return home. It was unbelievable. She was totally shocked that he took her words literally and went away for weeks. So, as a rule, avoid "*love fights*" and be careful what you say during those fights. Also, avoid heated arguments with a man as much as you can in your marriage because it won't get you the results you want, and he may not get the point. Men, generally, value peace. If a man feels like his peace is threatened the Bible tells us he will find an escape route.

Better to live on a corner of the roof than share a house with a quarrelsome wife. -Proverbs *25:24[NIV]*

Better to live alone in a tumbledown shack than share a mansion with a nagging spouse. -Proverbs *21:9 [TPT]*

It is such a serious thing to note that it was mentioned in the Bible more than once.

Men Are Created To Lead

You must have noticed this in your relationship with the man in your life. Leadership for a man is an inbuilt quality. Every woman has the capacity to influence a man. However, you must be careful not to *manipulate* your husband into doing things that will hurt your family. You must be careful not to fall into this temptation. The reason for this is simple; the man is the head of the home. This is not my personal opinion it is what the word of God says.

But I would have you know, that the head of every man is Christ; and the head of the woman is the man; and the head of Christ is God. -1st Corinthians 11:3 [NKJV]

For the husband is the head of the wife, even as Christ is the head of the church: and he is the savior of the body. -Ephesians 5:23 [KJV]

It says that the man is the head. The man—not the richer one, the smarter one, the stronger one, or even the one with more qualifications but ***"the man"***. The man is the head of the home.

Some women have destroyed their families by forcefully taking over the reins of leadership in their homes. Sometimes, you will be confronted with situations where you will find it very tempting to take over the decision making in your home, especially when the man is taking his time to make a decision over something that you think should be easy to handle. But do not do it because you are not authorized or anointed for it. Eve fell for this temptation. After she ate the fruit, she also convinced Adam to eat the fruit.

And when the woman saw that the tree was good for food, and that it was pleasant to the eyes, and a tree to be desired to make one wise, she took of the fruit thereof, and did eat, and gave also unto her husband with her; and he did eat. -Genesis 2:16-17 [KJV]

They both would have been saved a lot of stress if she had simply submitted to Adam's leadership and they had done what God had told Adam to do.

If you are married to a man who is given to procrastination, you need to pray that God will help him overcome his weakness, for grace to be patient through the process and for wisdom to take wise actions. If what you need him to do is something that you can initiate while he steps in to complete it, you can start doing it. But, if it is something that he has to do by himself then, pray about it and remind him about it once in a while.

MANAGING YOUR MAN

One of the things I need you to do as a woman is **to take your life more seriously.** God has invested so much in you. Right from when He created you, He used one of his finest materials. He took the most polished bone out of Adam. But Adam, He made from dirt; from dust. That should tell you something about your worth and value. God designed you specifically for a unique purpose and it is crucial that you discover it and function in it. To play your role effectively, you need to be happy and fulfilled. But the enemy will come after your happiness and fulfillment because he cannot afford to let you be all that God has created you to be. He is out to get you. He knows that you are very important in the grand scheme of things so he seeks to destroy you in any that he can knowing that a woman who is living up to her own potential is powerful.

He also knows that you are made for relationships, he will attack you the most through that aspect of your life. But if you are armed with the right knowledge, you will be immune to his schemes. In this chapter I will share with you the kinds of things you must be careful not to do in your relationship with men. These are mistakes many women make for various reasons that inevitably bring them very undesirable results in the end. Know them and be careful to avoid them. Keep this in mind; Relationships do not happen to you as a woman. Too many women respond to relationships as though there is very little they can do to impact their relationships positively. This is a very unhealthy way to view relationships. While it is true that a woman should submit to the leadership of her husband in a marital relationship, she should also bear in mind that she is largely responsible for choosing who leads her and ultimately the outcome of her relationship. You need to determine and be decisive about what you can and cannot accept in a relationship.

DO NOT ENTER A BAD RELATIONSHIP!

A bad relationship is worse than no relationship.

Some women tend to believe that it is better to be in a bad relationship than to be in none at all. This is an extremely dangerous mentality. I do not know of any ideology more detrimental to the total wellbeing of a women than this. If you have this mindset, you need to drop it immediately. It is true that women are more relationship-oriented than men, so it seems to be a need however, you are better off single until the right man comes along. Contrary to what you think, it can never be better to be in a bad relationship than to have no relationship. There is a vast difference between your natural inclination and what you should do. Everyone gets thirsty but no one drinks dirty water to quench his or her thirst. That is what makes us different from animals - our ability to control our desires and feelings. So just because you need to be in a relationship or are afraid of being single doesn't mean you should be in a bad relationship.

A lot of women are in unhappy marriages because they just can't be alone. They would rather hold on to what is not working instead of waiting for the real one. The woman in a bad relationship knows that the man she is with is not a good man. He abuses her physically, emotionally and verbally. He has no job, no money, and no ambition. Yet, she holds on to him instead of waiting for a good man. She keeps telling herself that she will leave him once she gets a better man not knowing that the fact that she chose to be in an abusive relationship will hinder her chances of ever this kind of thinking will hinder her chances of ever getting a good man. A man will recognize an unavailable woman even if he has not spoken a word to her.

As a woman, you give off a vibe or emotional energy that says something about you even before you open your mouth. Every woman carries an aura. Some women carry an atmosphere that they are emotionally unavailable even when they desire to be in a relationship. These women cannot attract the right men because they are taken. They are in a relationship with someone they do not like and who does not want them. They would rather manage him as he is or encourage themselves with the possibility that they can change him Do not hold onto someone that you know deep down in your heart is not good for you because you think you must be in a relationship whether you are happy in it or not. If you are single, be single. Be truly single. Be as single as possible. It helps your chances of meeting someone who will be good for you.

Every relationship you enter into makes a deposit in your life. You pick up something from each person you date that will affect your general disposition to life, especially in marriage. Knowing this, you now realize that it is better not to date anyone until you are ready to get married.

A lot of married women today are not happy in their marriages because they keep comparing their husbands to someone they used to know. When a woman says that sex with her husband is not good, it is usually because she has a point of reference. She is comparing him to someone else, physical or imaginary. Let me give you an example: if you eat a meal for the very first time in your life, the experience becomes your general idea of how the meal tastes and how it should taste. The only way you can tell that a plate of this particular meal is not delicious is if you have tasted another recipe prepared by someone else.

Careless dating for any young woman is a set up for marital failure. God designed that a married couple will grow in sexual intimacy with each other, as their marriage gets older. There is a general notion that men prefer to marry women who were sexually active as single ladies because they have a higher potential of satisfying them sexually in marriage. This is a deception from the pit of hell. What actually happens most times is that both parties develop appetites for sexual practices that do not interest the person they eventually get married to or they nurse unrealistic expectations their spouses are unable to live up to leaving them dissatisfied and sexually frustrated in their marriages.

DO NOT GIVE FREE SEX!

Most men want sex and not relationship

The wedding process from planning to execution doesn't excite a man half as much as it excites a woman. The average man would simply endure the process while his wife enjoys every bit of it. He can't wait to get to the sex on the wedding night and if he could skip the whole process to get to that part, he would gladly do it.

Sex is such a powerful thing that God never intended for anyone to engage in it outside the marriage covenant. God made man with a higher sexual passion than women. His plan was for the man's sexual passion to motivate him to get married at the right time. This is a foolproof plan if women would cooperate with God by denying men easy access to their bodies outside marriage. If only single ladies worldwide would unanimously agree to a 'no-sex-before-marriage' culture, the eligible bachelor's population will significantly reduce as more men would get married within a short period of time. The reason they remain unmarried is because they are sexually satisfied.

The average man with means would prefer to stay single while having multiple sexual partners. It is a carnal man's fantasy to enjoy sex with more than one woman. Knowing this, you sabotage yourself by giving out free sex to a man who is not your husband. If he is already getting it for free, there will be no motivation put a ring on it. As they say, "why buy the cow when the milk is free?" If a man wants to start a relationship with you, please do not be available for casual dating. This sets you up to be used because there is no clear definition of the relationship and what direction it is headed. A man can tell you anything just so he can get to sleep with you. He knows that you are vulnerable when it comes to love and marriage, so he wants to take advantage of you. Do not fall for it.

DO NOT BE DECEIVED!

A fornicator is an adulterer Trainee

Most single women tend to believe that once a man has promised to marry them, it is okay to have sex with him. But the truth is, when you engage in sexual activities with your fiancé before marriage, what you are really doing is breeding an adulterer. If a fornicator is like a tadpole, an adulterer is a full-grown frog. Do not coach or train your fiancé to have an appetite for illicit sex (sex outside marriage) or what the Bible calls *stolen waters.*

Stolen water is sweet. And bread eaten in secret is pleasant. -Proverbs 9:17 [ESV]

This is because even after he gets married to you, he will face the temptation to satisfy that appetite he has developed with you for stolen pleasures. Do not set yourself up like that. Decide from the beginning that you will not have sex before marriage.

In case you are worried that a man might leave you if you refuse to sleep with him, I'll let you in on a little secret; ***No man who really loves you will leave you because you denied him of sex before marriage.*** A man will stay with you because he loves you and not because he had sex with you. In a man's world love and sex are two separate things.

The primary intention of most men that want to date you is to have sex with you. Everything they do for you is to get you to have sex with them as soon as possible. If you want to distinguish the serious suitors from the unserious ones, it is very simple: ***just cut out the sex.*** If you are a single woman reading this, learn to *define every relationship that comes your way.* Once you do this, the time wasters will stay away from you. If you are a born-again Christian, you already know the standards. God says, 'No sex before marriage.'

Put to death, therefore, whatever belongs to your earthly nature: sexual immorality, impurity, lust, evil desires and greed, which is idolatry. **- Colossians 3:5 [NIV]**

So, do not sell yourself short thinking that you can keep a man by sleeping with him. That has never worked, and it will never work.

Some women honestly believe that sleeping with a man outside of marriage is an expression of how much they love each other. She thinks so because naturally, a woman would do anything for the man she loves but it is not so with the man. A man who is eager to sleep with a woman before he marries her is merely satisfying his lust. He is after the sexual pleasure he is getting from her. If you do a background check, you will discover that she is not his first and she certainly won't be his last. Even if they get married to each other eventually, she would assume that the end has justified the means but what she does not know is that his appetite for illegal sex rages on. By that time, she will no longer be the one who stirs his passions because now that they are married and legal, the thrill and excitement of secrecy is all gone. He would rather go out and hunt. Remember, ***nobody lusts after what they have***. Once, you get what you are lusting after, you quit lusting after it. The man that you are cheating with is really not on the same page with you.

Men are very determined creatures. If a guy is interested in you and makes a move to sleep with you and you tell him, 'Oh, I don't mess around like that,' he will value you for keeping yourself, even if he doesn't tell you that. With standards like that, even after you are both married, he will trust you to be faithful especially when he is not around. Most women who complain that their husbands accuse them of cheating were women who cheated with those same men when they were single. And now that they are married, their husbands simply cannot trust them.

DO NOT UNDERESTIMATE ACCOUNTABILITY!

Men Learn from Men

It takes a man to raise a man. As a rule, **never** start a relationship with a man that is not accountable to anyone.

If he was not accountable to someone before he met you, let him know ahead that you are a child of God with proper spiritual upbringing which means that apart from your physical parents, you belong to a spiritual family; a church. So, he needs to also meet with your pastors for accountability.

When a man hears this, he may not like the idea and might probably resist it at first but if he really wants to be with you, he will go through with it. So, make sure that the man you are about to marry or is married to has somebody over his life that talks to him. It makes a world of difference and it will bring you peace in the end.

Because you are fundamentally different from a man, it implies that he is usually not on the same page with you. So, when a situation where you both find it difficult to understand each other arises, he will need a stronger male figure that he respects to bring him to a frame of mind where he can hear you by showing him how to handle situations like that. Men have a lot of physical energy and they need to understand that the energy is not meant for bullying their wives but for protecting and providing for her. If your husband or fiancé does not have this kind of person in his life, he may not be able to reach his full potential and may never love you the way he should.

A spiritual authority can also tell if the man you call your fiancé is serious or if he is just there to waste your time. He will ask questions that will help you see the true nature of the man you are in a relationship with. When things are not going so well, you can nag a man for as long as you want over a matter and it won't make a difference but a man he respects could tell him just one word on that same issue and it will gain more mileage than all your nagging of several years put together. I will explain this with a story I once heard about a young elephant that was brought into a wildlife conservation. The young elephant was very big and strong. In a short while, it began to attack the rhinos in its environment. After some deliberation, the owners of the park decided to consult a specialist to analyze the situation. The specialist recommended that they bring in an older elephant that could show the younger elephant how elephants behave around rhinos. Once the older elephant arrived, the young elephant began to follow it around. Soon, it learned by observation that elephants do not attack rhinos and that ended the attack on rhinos in the park. The point of this story is that a man must have a strong person he is accountable to who can talk sense to him when necessary.

A man can be self-destructive if you leave him to his own devices. That is why he needs a woman in his life. So, when you are considering a man for marriage, ensure that he has a mentor: an authority figure over his life that can show him the importance of being family oriented. He needs to be trained to be the kind of man he needs to be. He needs a life coach who can talk to him when he is out of line. Having someone over his life will serve as a control switch to the power that you will give him over you when you accept to marry him.

DO NOT MARRY AN UNGODLY MAN!

He cannot love you if he does not love God.

Your security in a relationship lies in the fact that your man loves God more than he loves you. Most times, women focus on things such as "He loves me and can't do without me" which is not bad in itself. Your husband or fiancé should love you but that will not matter when the chips are down. We have already established that men are not in touch with their emotions as women are so whether he loves you more now or not, things are going to change radically when you marry him. One year in marriage and five years in marriage are very different stages of life. Don't be preoccupied with how much he loves you, ensure that he loves God.

You see, ***a man needs to love God to act right.*** Even if he doesn't love you, he will treat you right if he loves God. And the truth is that every man needs the help of the Holy Spirit to love a woman the way a woman should be loved.

God never told the woman to love her husband, it is the men He told, "***Love your wife***." (See Ephesians 5:25) From then until now, only a few men have come to understand what God was talking about. Make sure that the man you choose loves God.

HELPING YOUR MAN

Although most men are strong, they are not sufficient in themselves. Like every good device, they require accessories. That is why God in His infinite wisdom created the woman as a suitable and adaptable ***help for the man.***

Then the LORD God said, "It is not good for the man to be alone. I will make a helper who is just right for him." —Genesis 2:18 [NLT]

Most women have no idea how gifted and powerful they are. I usually tell women that your entrance into a man's life should move him into his kingship because a woman is a carrier of favor. Yes, you are that powerful.

A virtuous woman is a crown to her husband:...

- Proverbs 12:4 [KJV]

When a man finds a wife, he has found a treasure.

- Proverbs 18:22 [TPT]

Every woman has some natural gifting that can help a man achieve all his dreams and God-ordained purpose. These are the accessories that God has given to you as a woman that you can gift him with in order to make his life more useful, versatile and attractive.

· The Gift of Fantasy

This gift refers to your God-given capacity to dream. It is what makes a woman marry a seemingly poor man and support him till he becomes great in life. I often encourage husbands to share their dreams with their wives because women see things from a very different perspective. What she has to say might be the game changer to the man's dreams. However, the downside of this gift is that sometimes a woman will use it as an excuse to marry a man that is not good for her with the hope that she would be able to change him. A woman in love will believe anything a man tells her. However, men are not good at pretending. If he shows you through his actions that he is a certain kind of man, please believe him and do not make any excuses for him.

A jobless or an unfaithful man will not change because you married him. He has built a pattern of infidelity or laziness and patterns are consistent. Somewhere in your mind you might think he's just going through a phase and will change with time. Well, here is some news for you ladies; ***Marriage does not change any man.*** Don't marry a man's potentials; marry his patterns. A violent man or a man without ambition will remain the same even after marriage. Do not marry a lazy man. ***Do not marry a man because of money; however, you should marry considering money.*** Always consider his financial habits because when all the intoxicating emotions of love is gone, harsh realities will set in. Many women today are stressed out by the tough financial times in their homes. They married someone they knew was lazy with the hope that he would change. Before you make that decision to be with him, ask yourself...

What has he been able to do with his life since he left school?

What trade has he learnt or what skills has he acquired?

What are his financial patterns and behaviors?

Is he deluding himself with the 'there are no jobs in the country' excuse?

If he has not been able to do anything in his many years of adulthood before you met him, chances are high that if you marry him, he will remain exactly the way you met him.

· **The Gift of Details**

Women have the capacity to pay attention to details than men. Ten men can live in a tiny apartment using each other's personal items and there will be no quarrel. But when you switch things up and leave just three women in this same setting, you are asking for trouble as each of them will have a list of instructions tied to everything she owns most of which can be quite unrealistic to adhere to. But women can understand this and keep all the instructions and rules because they are used to handling such details.

That is why in most cases, it is usually better that the woman runs the nitty gritty of the family's operations. Things like the family's finances are better managed by women generally. She knows where to cut off excesses and save for future investments. Her gift of detail makes her a better planner. However, if this gift is not properly handled, it will make a woman petty.

A petty woman will not know how to choose her battles especially with her husband. You cannot fight over everything. It is wise to save your energy for the real issues. You can't use that one shortcoming your husband has to be a source of constant irritation or else it will turn you into a bitter woman. Learn to choose your battles wisely and preserve your peace.

· The Gift of Perfection

The gift of perfection is necessary for one to enjoy a life of excellence and progress. Women like to see everything as perfect and that's a good thing. However, many women are unhappy in their marriages because things are not 100% perfect. The average woman strips herself completely of joy by comparing her marriage with that of someone else even when there is no basis for comparison. Life does not work that way. Sometimes, God needs you to be content and happy where you are and with what He has blessed you with. Do not let that aspect of your marriage that does not seem to be working the way you want it to work yet steal your joy.

Recently, one of my daughters in the Lord complained to me that she was unhappy in her marriage because her husband's lack of ambition was affecting their finances. So, I asked her a few questions, 'Before you got married to him, was he ambitious?

She said, 'No, Sir. He wasn't. But I had hopes that he would change.'

I probed further. 'Is he a good father?'

'Yes.' She replied, 'He is very caring, and the children love him.'

'Has he ever attempted to physically abuse you?'

'Never!' She replied.

'Do you think that he may be cheating on you?'

'No!' She replied emphatically.

Then I said to her, 'Count your blessings and be happy.'

She entered that relationship fully aware of the kind of person her husband was. And a few years into the marriage, she is frustrated by the fact that he was not responding to her attempts to change him. Women have a tendency to look for a problem where there is none. You need to guard against that perfectionist tendencies. Although you cannot train your husband or fiancé, you can be the push he needs to become a perfect representation of who God has made him to be.

Ask yourself, 'Can I do better in those areas that my husband is not great at yet?' If you can, then start doing better. God has blessed you already. When someone has a score of four out of five points, that is fair enough. Look at what is working in your marriage right now and thank God for it. Then, begin to think on how can make it even better. God has given every woman the gift of influence. You can influence your man into doing what is right and not what is wrong like Eve did to Adam. If you do not use your gifts right, the enemy will use it for you.

If you are single, it is okay to aim for five out of five in the man of your dreams or choose to settle for less, it is up to you. You have to decide whether you can live with him the way he is or not. Some women do not mind being the breadwinner in the family. They just want to keep the man. I do not support this in anyway, but I have seen it happen. If you know that it is important to you that a man is working and being a good role model to your children, then this kind of man is not for you.

For the married woman who is already living in her imperfect situation, please try to work with what you have to be happy. Getting out of your matrimonial home is never the best option. Get good counsel before making such a life-altering decision.

HAZARDS TO YOUR MAN

Certain things can destroy every device, and for a man it is infidelity. Infidelity is one of the major hazards that can destroy life. It can literally reduce him to nothing—a piece of bread. (See Proverbs 6:26). It is important that you understand the infidelity hazard: how it happens, why it happens and how you can help him overcome it and ensure that it never happens again.

It is hard to believe that a good woman, loving her husband, training her children and keeping her home can have her marriage threatened overnight by her husband's natural body changes. But that is what happens with infidelity. She can totally be blindsided, but a bit of information can help her become better prepared to deal with this menace that is silently seeping into a lot of homes. Let me share a few things that you must keep at the back of your mind.

Every Man is Tempted

A man's sexual drive has nothing to do with love. He can love his wife, have a great sex life with her and yet desire to sleep with someone else. This is one major temptation most men have to deal with. And it has been made worse by social media platforms where with just one click sex can be arranged between two complete strangers.
Most women can tell when their husbands are cheating. The signs are obvious. You may find that he is never fully present at any time or that he is always on his phone making endless calls beyond your earshot or that he is chatting away with someone that you do not know. Men can be likened to pack animals; a breed of animals that move together. So, if a good man starts to hang out with adulterers and fornicators often, the chances are that if he is not already living that life, eventually they will draw him into it. And when it comes to adultery, most men fall under these three major categories.

· ***The Random Adulterer***

This is kind of adultery is unplanned. In this case, a man can wake up in the morning with plans that has nothing to do with sex and by evening he has had sex with a total stranger. He did not plan it. He encountered the temptation in a moment of weakness, and he fell into it.

· ***The Flirt***

This involves a flirtatious man who actively pursues and seeks the attention of women everywhere he goes. He has no control over his passions. He sleeps with different kinds of girls at any chance he gets and anytime he feels like it.

· ***The Full-blown Adulterer***

This kind of adultery usually involves being in a full-time relationship with the other woman. The married man is emotionally attached to the woman he is cheating on his wife with. He is committed to her and keeps her as a 'side-chick'. He believes that they have a real relationship, even though in reality he is just hooked on the sex and attention he is getting from her while she is hooked on the money and gifts she is getting from him. Some men go as far as renting apartments and buying properties for these women.

If your spouse is involved in any form of adultery, it is important that you get help urgently. This will save him from destroying himself and the family.

Prostitutes reduce a man to poverty, and the adulteress steals your soul—she may even cost you your life! - **Proverbs 6:26 [TPT]**

You will find some of the steps you can take to help him in the latter part of this book.

Age Changes Men

Most men become more vulnerable to the plot of the other woman at an older age. This is because they become aware of a decline in their sexual passion and desire to keep it alive by all means. For most men, sleeping with one woman constantly for years can get boring and when this happens, it can lead to a gradual decline in a man's sexual passion.

Most men cannot accommodate this decline, so they start craving for a hunt. When a man at this stage gets a new sexual partner, he gets his sexual passion back temporarily. But this pattern will eventually become a trap for him because he will have to always change girls or keep a woman outside of his matrimonial home. The only thing that will stop a man at this stage from getting involved with another woman is if he has a relationship with God. I cannot overemphasize the need for your husband to have a relationship with God; it is the only factor that keeps you safe as a woman in marriage.

Consciously invest in being his friend, his help, so that he cannot do without you. Be an active part of his life, career, business or whatever he is involved in. You need to bring more to the marriage than just sex. If all you bring to the marriage is sex, you most likely will lose his full attention to other women at this stage of his life when you need him the most if he is not saved.

Dealing with Infidelity

- **Get help!**

If your heart has been broken by a cheating husband, please get help. Get counseling. Do not sit at home hurting and expect healing to happen to you. Open up to a trained counsellor who will walk you through the healing process. The process of healing, forgiving, moving on and eventually forgetting is a long one. You should not go through it alone. Like the Bible says:

Where no counsel is, the people fall: but in the multitude of counsellors there is safety.

- Proverbs 11:14[KJV]

Opening up to the right person will speed up the healing process and help you get all the negative emotions out of your system in a controlled environment. Remember, if you hurt yourself and you don't open the wound to dress it, there is no way the wound can heal, instead it will get worse. So, get help.

- **Forgive him**

Forgive your husband. You are not forgiving him because he deserves to be forgiven. You are forgiving him because you deserve to heal. There is no healing without forgiveness. Unforgiveness is extremely dangerous to both your physical and mental health. Studies have shown that many serious health issues are traceable to unforgiveness. The pain of betrayal can hurt very deeply but you must be willing to forgive your husband. It is through forgiveness that all the negative emotions you feel towards him can pour out of your soul and trust me, you need a soul detox. I must tell you this, only God can help you with forgiving him. You have to ask for His help and be willing to receive it. Unforgiveness is like drinking poison and expecting someone else to die.

Get rid of all bitterness, rage and anger, brawling and slander, along with every form of malice. Be kind and compassionate to one another, forgiving each other, just as in Christ God forgave you."

- Ephesians 4:31-32[NIV]

He will make more progress knowing that you can forgive him and not always put his sins in his face. It is important to note that your healing is key in this process because if after he is restored and he sees that you are still in pain, it will hurt him more and even make him feel ashamed. A man who is dealing with shame cannot be the man he is meant to be.
So, allow the Holy Spirit to help you. Look for someone you can talk to, preferably, a pastor, a spiritually mature woman or a therapist who can walk you through the process.

The fact that he committed adultery is not your fault, it was his choice. But it would also be a good idea to use this opportunity to check your own self. Have you been doing everything right by your husband? Are there ways you can also make adjustments in how you relate with him? The truth is, none of us are perfect, so ask God to show you aspects of your life where you can do better in your marriage. Then, forgive yourself if you feel like there is a way you may have contributed to his straying. The essence of this is not to make you feel bad but to get you to be the best version of yourself. You are stronger than you know, and you can actually make it through this phase of your life.

- **Pray for him**

Until you can pray for your husband, you have not really forgiven him. I know you were deeply hurt and broken by his infidelity but do not let unforgiveness live in your heart. It will harm you. Your husband needs your prayers. Adultery destroys men. A cheating husband is not just cheating on his wife, but he is destroying his very own life. His destiny is under attack. So, he needs your prayers. The Bible says:
Whoever commits adultery with a woman lacks understanding;

He who does so destroys his own soul. - Proverbs 6:32 [NKJV]

Do not give your strength to women, nor your ways to that which destroys kings. -Proverbs 31:3 [NKJV]

No man in his right senses commits adultery. An adulterous man loses the very essence of his life and destiny as long as that adulterous relationship lasts. So, he needs you. Try not to be the prosecutor or the judge rather be his defender, even though you can see all the ways he could have done better. You can draw strength from God, a strong support system of godly women and mentors as you pray for him. You can also draw strength from the fact that you are fighting for your children. You want them to grow up in a healthy home with both parents loving each other.

You can fight for your marriage with prayers. God can reach him through your prayers for his soul. Trust God to convict him and expose his sinful life to him. This is very important because sin thrives in secrecy.

Suspicion has never stopped any man from committing adultery and accusing him will only put him in a defensive mode. If you accuse him, his first instinct will be to deny it. If you monitor and try to track him because you suspect him, he will only get smarter in hiding what he does. Men find it difficult to open up.

For that reason, they never really get healed from the things they go through. His sinful life needs to be exposed for healing to take place.

You will never succeed in life if you try to hide your sins. Confess them and give them up; then God will show mercy to you. -Proverbs 28:13 [GNT]

If he can open up either to you or to the authority figures in his life, then he can get help. Therefore, getting him to open up is vital. And if you stand with God in faith, God will expose him in a way that everything will work out for your good. However, you must be patient for God to act. Resist that temptation to try to answer your own prayer. God is on your side. Let Him fight your battle.

The LORD himself will fight for you. Just stay calm. -Exodus 14:14 [NLT]

- **Help him**

Now, ask yourself, "What can I start doing differently to help his restoration?" A man at this stage needs to learn to love his wife differently and you can help him do that by paying attention to him and what interests him. He needs to learn to appreciate and connect with you more intellectually, functionally and emotionally than sexually. So, get involved in his life. Find ways to engage him and make him enjoy your company more. Have good and deep conversations with him. This will make him desire you more and fuel his sexual passion towards you. He needs to be taught by those he is accountable to that he has to carry out his conjugal duties to you even when he is not in the mood. And when he falls in love with you again, not for your body but for your impact in his life, you would have gotten your man back.

· **Establish structures**

Men have a high tendency to stray and every man is going to battle this tendency at one point or the other in his life. This is why I advise men, long before they get married, to have a mentor they submit to. And like I have already told you; your husband needs to have someone who empowers him to see a possible future and benefits of a faithful marriage. The right mentor for your husband must be a godly man whose marriage is working according to God's Manual. This mentor will show him the ropes on how to secure his marriage from the ravages of adultery. It is one thing to get him back from the bondage of adultery, however it is more important to set boundaries to keep him from falling prey to such wayward ways. You might be able to spot a potentially dangerous relationship fast and not be able to communicate it to him but a mentor he looks up to and respects may tell him only once and he will make the necessary adjustments.

I cannot overemphasize the importance of not risking your life with a man who is not submitted to authority. Such a man will self-destruct. Even as the lead pastor of a church, my wife is at liberty to go to my mentors whenever she finds it difficult to get through to me on any matter and she has had to use that liberty a few times. It is for my own good. With the help of your spiritual authorities, you can get him to agree to put in structures that will safeguard him against possible temptations in the future. Even the devil after he tempted Jesus, left him for just a while.

***When the devil had finished tempting Jesus, he left him until the next opportunity came.* - Luke 4:13 [NLT]**

With your husband's permission, you can also set up accountability structures like syncing your phones. This will give you access to his messages especially on social media applications. My wife and I have our phones synchronized so she can see all my chats.

MY ADVICE TO WOMEN

I'm sure by now you know how much your man needs you to be the best you can be and in case the man in your life does not tell you how much he values your input as often as you would want him to, you now know that the reason is because men are not as expressive as women are. Personally, I try my best to make sure that my wife knows exactly how much she means to me and I can tell you that saying it often doesn't come naturally to me, but I have had to learn over the years. God is helping those of us who are willing to accept His help. Most men know that there is not much they can do without you. Unfortunately, many women are unaware of the power they have and so they keep chasing after the same people who should be chasing after them. If only you would spend that time chasing God.

· **Put God First**

Your marriage, finances, career, business and everything else is affected first by your relationship with God.

I feel a lot of women, whether married or single, exert too much energy focusing on and worrying about men. Remember that marriage is God's idea. Every man was created by God, so you need God's wisdom to relate properly with him. You can get this wisdom through an active relationship with God. As a matter of fact, your marriage, finances, career, business and everything else is affected by your relationship with God. You can trust God with your life. He will never leave you stranded. He knows the way when you don't. And if there is no way, He will make one because He is the Way Maker. Feel free to ask Him for the wisdom you need to move your relationship forward. The wisdom of God helps us to address the most important issues in dealing with relationships.

If you don't know what you're doing, pray to the Father. He loves to help. You'll get his help and won't be condescended to when you ask for it. Ask boldly, believingly, without a second thought…
- James 1:5-6[MSG]

In fact, most of the issues women face in their relationships are linked to a lack of wisdom. I can't count how many times I have had to counsel women on little things that God's Word (wisdom) has addressed. Things such as responding gently in order to avoid heated fights with their husbands;

Respond gently when you are confronted, and you'll defuse the rage of another. Responding with sharp, cutting words will only make it worse. Don't you know that being angry can ruin the testimony of even the wisest of men? -Proverbs 15:1[TPT]

Or marrying unbelievers;

Do not be unequally bound together with unbelievers [do not make mismatched alliances with them, inconsistent with your faith]. For what partnership can righteousness have with lawlessness? Or what fellowship can light have with darkness? What harmony can there be between Christ and Belial (Satan)? Or what does a believer have in common with an unbeliever? *-2nd Corinthians 6:14-15[AMP]*

An unbeliever does not have the ability to treat you right. In fact, he does not have the ability to love you the way God has commanded him to. So, building your relationship with God will help you understand what love truly is and in turn help you decide what is acceptable or unacceptable in a relationship. This is critical in order to help you avoid pitfalls like this in marriage and save you a lot of heartache.

· **Build your Dreams**

Most women sacrifice their dreams on the altar of marriage

Do not abandon your dreams or career because you are waiting to be married. It is one of the worst mistakes any woman can make. Many women are not striving to be great in life. They just want to get married. What they don't realize is that a woman is more attractive to a man, especially as a married woman, when she is actively doing something with her life. Your husband cannot be all that your life is about. A man needs his space. You cannot talk to him or be in his face all day. Get yourself a dream; something you are passionate about and get busy making a difference in the world with it.

If you are single, listen to this: ***one of the ways you make people interested in you is by being interesting.*** This means that there has to be some interesting things you are involved with for someone to find you interesting. You can't just be preoccupied with getting married. Consciously build a career, go to school or learn a trade.

Do not forfeit your career because of a man. You'll be doing yourself a great disservice by putting your life on hold to please a man or get him to marry you. It is very unlikely that he would do the same for you, so get a life. What if he wakes up one day and decides to walk out on you and the relationship? Being heartbroken is bad but being heartbroken and broke is much worse. If you are heartbroken but not broke, you can afford chocolates and ice cream to cry over. You may even decide to go on a vacation or go shopping to clear your mind and heal.

Two things can trap a woman: greed or lack but making your own money helps you escape these traps. Greed is why a lady who has no source of income will do everything possible to sustain an appetite for expensive things. Men who want to take advantage of you can sense this so they will come with tempting offers knowing that you cannot resist or afford your cravings. Some women think they are being smart by spending a man's money without giving him anything in return. That's just greed at work. It is more dignifying to make and spend your own money.

Lack, on the other hand, is the state of being without or not having enough of something. I understand that some women are in a genuine state of lack and some men are willing to prey on some of these young women at the cost of having carnal knowledge of them. These women are not bad people, but they simply don't have the basic necessities of life like what to eat, what to wear and where to live and will do anything to have these needs met. The point is, greed or lack will put you in a weak position with any man. So, build a life for yourself. When you are asked what your dream is, you should be able to state it clearly. Don't just sit down and wait for a man to bail you out of poverty. Marriage should not be a financial plan. Go and make your own money and foot your own bills. You are more attractive when you are not a liability. There is nothing honorable about bringing only sex to the table. Do something with your life. Live your dream. It's uncommon to see a man shutting down his dreams for a woman but a woman will throw away everything she's worked for just to win the love of a man. Do not shut down your life or your dreams. Live your best life now.

Conclusion

If after you have read this book you feel a little more hopeful about your relationships with men, then I would have achieved my aim of writing it. I believe that in spite of our fundamental differences, God expects men and women to find a way to live together. And that is what this book is about; to help you embrace the fact that although a man might seem easy on the surface, there is a whole lot going on in his mind that influences his behavior towards you. Your knowledge of these unique nature of a man will help you connect deeper with him as you become more functionally stimulating and irresistible to him.

By now you also realize that developing yourself to your full potential is a major factor in this and you need God's help with that.

If you already have a relationship with God, you can go ahead and ask Him for help with your man. But if you don't, now is the best time to start a fully rewarding relationship with Him. Just say this prayer with me;

Lord Jesus, I come to you today. I acknowledge that I am a sinner and I believe that you came, died and rose again to save me. I open my heart to you and ask that you be my Lord and Savior from today onwards. [Romans 10:9-10].

Thank you, Lord, for saving me and transforming me into your kingdom. I receive the power to serve you all the days of my life. In Jesus Name. Amen.

OTHER BOOKS BY KINGSLEY & MILDRED OKONKWO

WHO SHOULD I MARRY?
25 WRONG REASONS WHY PEOPLE ENTER INTO RELATIONSHIP
WHEN AM I READY?
JUST US GIRLS
I OVE YOU BUT MY PARENTS SAY NO
GOD TOLD ME TO MARRY YOU
SHOULD LADIES PROPOSE?
WAITING FOR ISSAC
CHAYIL- THE VIRTUOUS WOMAN
7 QUALITIES WISE MEN WANT
7 QUESTIONS WISE WOMEN ASK
A-Z OF MARRIAGE
CHAYIL- PRAYER JOURNAL
HANNAH'S HEART
ALL YEAR ROUND FOR MEN
ALL YEAR ROUND FOR WOMEN
HELP, MY HUSBAND IS ACTING FUNNY

About the Author

Kingsley Okonkwo is the senior Pastor of David's Christian Centre in Lagos. A profound teacher with a passion for building strong marriages based on timeless biblical principles.

He is the host of the popular monthly relationship seminar, Love, Dating and Marriage, which currently airs weekly on television stations. He is a much sort after speaker whose humor and practical styled teachings have been a blessing to people of all ages and races.

He is happily married to his lovely wife and best friend Mildred who pastors with him and they have three lovely children together.

Made in United States
North Haven, CT
28 April 2025

68415527R00049